"How to Guide"

Personal Spiritual Development Analysis

Rick & Coral Gray

Acknowledgment

This book is dedicated with gratitude to Dr. Robert Clinton and to all who are on an intentional quest to discover God's purpose for their existence and present circumstances.

You are not an accident.

GrayceBook Publishing
8980 Palos Verde Drive
Orlando, FL 32825

World Wide Web: www.GrayceBook.com

E-mail: grayrick1@gmail.com

© *2008 by Rick Gray*

All rights reserved. No part of this book may be reproduced, distributed or transmitted in any form without the prior written permission from GrayceBook Publishing, except in the case of brief quotations embodied in critical reviews and other non-commercial uses permitted by copyright law.

Printed in the United States of America

Cover artwork was produced from a photo taken by Coral Gray within a cave at Masada during a 2008 trip to the Holy Land.

Part One: The Title Page

Develop a heading that identifies this study as a spiritual autobiography. Consider a statement like "An intimate look into the spiritual journey of. . ." or simply "Personal Spiritual Development Analysis."

Part Two: Expanded Personal Biography

Is comprised of demographic information about yourself that will help locate your age, gifts, etc.

Part Three: The Personal Timeline

This is a continuum that begins with the date of your birth and flows to the present time. It is a structured picture of the major transition points, secondary transition points and formative encounters of your life.

Part Four: The Snapshot

This is a single spaced 3 to 5 page narrative that provides a picture of your journey – to date.

Part Five: The Formative Encounter

Formative Encounters are those people, activities, events or anything else God uses in the spiritual development of a person.

Part Six: The Discovery Statement

This statement should be a one-page indication of the significant learning from doing this study.

Part Seven: A Sample PSDA

Introduction

The Personal Spiritual Development Analysis is designed to help you know that God has been at work within you, molding and shaping you spiritually, from a time long before you embraced him. This exercise will help you to see that he actually began the work of forming you even before you knew that he cared for and loved you.

Your personal spiritual development analysis is a personal spiritual timeline of your life from early childhood to today. However, rather than trying to write a spiritual autobiography of your entire life, limit your reflections to those events which have had special significance to your faith walk and spiritual formation. You are to identify key events in your life, recast these events as "formative encounters," and apply a spiritual significance to the event as a lesson learned (see the example provided). By breaking the events of your life down into formative encounters (single significant events) and giving a spiritual significance to that event, you will begin to see how God is using the events in your life to shape you. This understanding should help you understand that there are deep reasons for the events of our lives.

As you develop your PSDA, you will find yourself reliving memories of events that have been very formational in your personal development. Permit yourself to pray, laugh, cry and even heal where necessary as the Holy Spirit guides you back across your life's experiences. Some memories no doubt will be painful and some may cause feelings of shame or regret. Don't dwell on the negatives but rather permit the Holy Spirit to help you look beyond them to see how God has always been standing at your side guiding you to this very moment. Take comfort in this knowledge and be assured that "God has begun a good work in you and will perform it until the day of Jesus Christ." (Phil. 1:6).

1

The Title Page

Begin your PSDA by completing a title page. Consider including pictures to make the page more interesting and personal. The next page will give you an idea of what your title page should look like. Remember to be creative. Your title page does not have to look exactly like the sample.

*The Personal
Spiritual Development
Analysis*

of

[Your Name]

Date:

2

Expanded Personal Biography

Your personal biography will provide demographic information to anyone who may read your study at a later date. It will also help you remember when your spiritual autobiography was first undertaken as you add to it in later years.

You do not have to limit yourself to the demographic headings that have been suggested. Include any additional heading and information that you think will be helpful knowledge for someone reading this study at a later date.

Expanded Personal Biography

Date information compiled for this study:

Name:

Current Age:

Personal Time-Line Dates:

You do not have to limit yourself to these headings. They represent the minimal information in your finished study.

Date this study was completed:
Age when I embraced Jesus Christ as Savior:

Age when I discovered my Spiritual Gift(s)

Spiritual Gifts mix:

Primary gift   _____
Secondary gift   _____
Secondary gift   _____
Secondary gift   _____

Talents:

Primary talent   _____
Secondary talent _____

Major roles I've occupied:

Sample Expanded Personal Biography

Name: Gifted Christ Follower
Current Age: XX
Timeline Dates: Sept. 1949 – Aug. 2015
Date Study Was Completed: Summer 2015
Age When I Embraced Jesus Christ As Savior: 15 Age
When I Discovered My Spiritual Gifts: 19

Spiritual Gifts Mix:
Primary Gift: Teaching
Secondary Gift: Administration,
Tertiary Gift: Mercy, Pastoring

Talents:
Primary Talent: Teaching
Secondary Talent: Public speaking
Major Roles I've Occupied:
 Student, Pastor Husband, Teacher

Ministry Area:
 Meadville, PA; Indianapolis, IN; Pasadena, CA; Ft. Wayne, IN; Wilmore, KY; Orlando, FL;

Major Roles Occupied:
High School Football and Wrestling Star; Leader in Urban Ministry Outreach Program; Leader in Social Justice Outreach Program; Business Owner; Writer; Professor; Leader in National Ministry Outreach Programs

3

The Personal Timeline

Your personal timeline should be constructed as a continuum drawn along a horizontal line and not as a vertical dyad. Pay close attention to the example provided.

⟵――――――――⟶

Constructing a Personal Timeline.

Your time line should have a beginning date. Have it begin with your birth and establish a new date for each Major Developmental Era. Once you have your Major Transition Points identified and located on the time line, you will need to give each a heading. For example your earliest Formative Encounter might have occurred while you were a child growing up in your parents' home. You would understand this to be a part of your early formational period. Locate this period and give it a heading to reflect its significance. In our example below, *Foundational Base* represents the first developmental paradigm or early formational period. *Ministry Validation Through Preparation* represents the second paradigm and *Growing Influence* represents the third paradigm.

In *The Making of a Leader*, Clinton identifies six major phases. They serve as a helpful guide. We took Clinton's six phases and collapsed them down to three major paradigms to more accurately reflect the development of this writer. You should do the same.

Next, locate the secondary transition points in your life. A transition point is a significant happening that caused a changing of the direction your life was going. Examples of transition points include: conversion experience, going off to college, relocation, getting married, etc. We all have those pivotal points in our experiences. Once you have identified your personal transition points, give them a title unique to your life.

Major and Secondary Transition Points

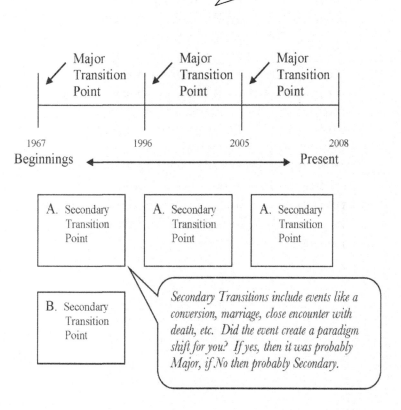

Note that the Foundational Base paradigm has two sections. Section A contains all of those formation encounters that were important for helping this individual through infancy and early adolescence. The event which separated section A from section B was a conversion experience and section B contains all of those formation encounters which helped shape this person's early Christian walk. Combined, these transition headings, along with the titles you give your major developmental eras will form the titles for the SnapShot.

Major Developmental & Secondary Transition Headings

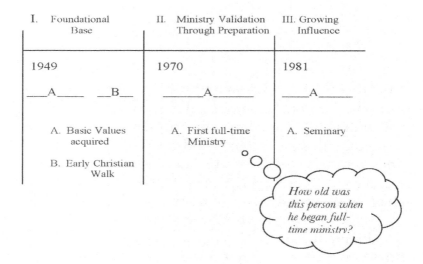

Note: You can tell the age of the individual when the transitions occurred. Also, note how the headings of the various transitions have been personalized to this particular individual. You can also tell that this person was 32 years old when he entered seminary. The last formative encounter under the Ministry Validation Through Preparation section of this study should help us to understand why the paradigm shift occurred.

the Timeline

ed your major
ns, identified the dates
egan and sectioned each era,
your age into the time line.
age at the beginning of each
new ___ aradigm and the location
where the maj___ the formation encounters
occurred.

Age	21	32	38
Location	Hometown	Indianapolis, IN	Dallas, TX

Note that it was a change in location that aided in the shift from one paradigm to the next.

Listing Formative Encounters

Next on your PSDA is the actual inclusion of your headings for your *Formative Encounters*.

A1. Grandma	A1. YFC	A1. Seminary
A2. Sunday School	A2. First Boss	A2. Pannell
A3. The 4 horsemen	A3. Jubilation I	A3. L.C.W.E.
A4. Jr. High English	A4. The Center	
B1. Lifeline Camp		
B2. Bible Quizzing		
B3. The "Bird"		

Usually the last Encounter in a paradigm speaks to why one era ends and another one begins.

These Encounters flow in chronological order. Where an event spans a long period of time, locate it where it had the greatest spiritual impact.

Note the lettering and numbering of the Formative Encounters and how they relate to the Transition Points on the Timeline. There is no limit on the number of Formative Encounters that you can identify but you probably won't want to have less than 30. The Formative Encounters are centered around the context, events and people who have been significant in your spiritual journey thus far. You should write out the story of the event in one page or less. Remember to leave space at the bottom of the page to make a spiritual application for the lesson (how did this event help shape you spiritually? Is there a universal spiritual principle?) Formative Encounters flow in chronological order thru your life. Developmental Paradigms tend to overlap so be creative in labeling them. Make the titles reflective of your life's journey.

A Complete Personalized Timeline

I. Foundational Base	II. Ministry Validation Through Preparation	III. Growing Influence
1949 __A__ __B__	1970 _____A_____	1981 _____A_____
A. Basic Values Acquired B. Early Christian Walk	A. First full-time Ministry	A. Seminary
21 ▶	32 ▶	38 ▶
Hometown	Indianapolis, IN	Pasadena, CA
A1. Grandma A2. Sunday School A3. The 4 horsemen A4. Jr. High English B1. Lifeline Camp B2. Bible Quizzing B3. The "Bird"	A1. YFC A2. First Boss A3. Jubilation I A4. The Center	A1. Seminary A2. Pannell A3. L.C.W.E.

If reading this was all that a person was able to do, it should still give them a good picture of who you

The SnapShot

This is a single spaced 3 to 5 page narrative that provides a picture of your journey to-date.

By reading the SnapShot, one should gain an overview of the significant occurrences in your life. This overview should flow through your life chronologically.

We've included an entire SnapShot so that you can get a feel for the length and quality of the reflection.

> *Here is an example of a SnapShot. Note that this example is written in 1st person, you should write in 1st person as well. Note also how the title for each section exactly matches the Major Developmental and Secondary Transition titles in the Timeline.*

I. FOUNDATIONAL BASE

A. Basic Values

I was one of nine children born to my parents. I have four brothers and four sisters. We were never a close family in the traditional sense and the fact that we were a very poor Black family did not help. Even so, I can remember very definite efforts on the part of my parents to teach me some basic values that have helped shape me and carry me through life.

One such lesson occurred when I was five years old. Mother often sent me to the corner grocery store to buy items for a meal. The store was only a block from our home and there were no crosswalks between the store and our house, so it was a relatively safe trip. On one fateful expedition to purchase a loaf of bread, I also tarried in front of the candy counter long enough to spend some of my mother's change. This wasn't the first time I had done, so I didn't give it a thought as I walked home chewing my double bubble chewing gum. My mother was waiting for me as I walked through the front door. Before I had a chance to put the bread down, she was hovering over me. Her large hand held mine firmly and her eyes flared as she counted the change in my palm. I don't think it was the fact that I spent two cents that didn't belong to me, although I was made to understand that that was exactly what I had done, nor was it the fact that I spent the money on candy before dinner. Rather, her anger was kindled because I disappointed her. I didn't ask for permission first and for that reason, I had violated her trust. I was guilty of stealing. That lesson is still operative and powerful in my life.

There are many such lessons from my childhood. It now appears that they hung over me and have helped shield me from many of the pitfalls of adolescence.

B. Early Christian Walk

At age fifteen, I had a chance to attend a Youth For Christ sponsored camp. My attendance at this camp turned out to be a turning point in my life. I attended the camp with three friends from our neighborhood and during our time there, we were given all the food we could eat and all the sports we could play. We were also introduced to a routine of activities that were unlike any that I had known. At that camp, for the first time in my life, I saw people my own age reading the Bible outside of the church. Before the week was over we all had an opportunity to hear the testimonies of the camp's staff, some of whom were our peers and a number of the campers. One evening towards the end of our week at the camp, a bonfire was kindled and various individuals shared their testimonies. I was the only one of the gang who grew interested enough to remain behind and talk to the staff about the things they had shared. During our conversation, I shared for the first time my feelings of a prepared destiny for me. I shared my hunger and longing for the type of relationship with God that they were describing. They helped me to understand that such a relationship was only possible through Jesus Christ. I accepted Christ as my savior at the camp and knew immediately that my life had suddenly and permanently changed.

About the time that I became a Christian I also came into my own in sports. The Youth For Christ organization spotlighted me in their rallies and I soon had a reputation around the region as a serious Christ follower. As a Christ follower I was taught to carry my Bible on the top of my stack of books through the school each day as a testimony. By my senior year of high school my faith walk was well known and remained a mystery to many of my classmates. I was a high school jock and a Christian. It was the "Bird" who found enough courage to ask me about it one day at the beginning of a class.

The "Bird"

"I've been watching you for a while now and you're different from the days when we used to run together. Also, you carry that Bible on top of your books. Can you tell me what it's all about? What happened to you?"

I was totally unprepared for the bird's question. I had just sat down in a 12th grade English class. The questioner was Bob Boyer. We had spent the last two years of our elementary school days running the streets of our community together. It was there that he had earned his nickname: The Bird.

Bob liked to climb to the tops of trees and ride the branches as they bent down to the ground. We were both known as wild in those days, but lost contact when we started junior high school.

I now sat in my seat stunned. I was a high school football and wrestling star and, as a new Christian two years into the faith, had been trained to carry my Bible high and proud. No one had ever asked my why before.

I grew embarrassed at the attention we were receiving and put The Bird off, explaining that we would talk about it another time. In truth, I didn't know what to say to him. Bob and I would never again have an opportunity to talk about it. A few weeks before graduation, on the night of the prom, Bob tried to climb to the top of one of the highest trees in the woods while at a beer party. The branch broke off as he tried to ride it to the ground. He died instantly when his head hit the hard dirt. I have never forgotten that he one day asked me for a reason for my hope.

I got serious about the Word of God after that. I never again wanted to be embarrassed by someone asking me why I was different. Since that day, I've always felt that two people had to die for Rick Gray. The first died to save my soul, and the second, to make me get serious about my profession of faith. After the bird's death I began to study the scriptures and to learn for myself what the journey I had embraced was to mean for my living and conversation.

II. MINISTRY VALIDATION THROUGH PREPARATION

A. First Full-time Ministry

With the help of the Youth for Christ people, I attended a Bible School in Arizona and during each summer worked at a camp sponsored by the organization. The camp was very much like the camp where I had come to know Jesus Christ as Lord and Savior so I was comfortable with the role of athletic director that I was asked to play. Because the camp was located in Indiana, I transferred from the Bible School to Anderson College in Anderson, Indiana. It was a fateful transfer because I was soon approached by the YFC organization to their inner city clubhouse program that had been developed as a follow-up program for the kids that attended the camp during the summers.

I worked for eight years in that inner city clubhouse program and developed my initial ministry skills. I was introduced to basic administration and entry leadership development. I graduated from Anderson College during the time I worked at the Clubhouse and this only made me more valuable as an employee of Youth for Christ. The Clubhouse program was eventually written up in the organizations national magazine called *Campus Life*.

My development in ministry soon found me directing the Urban Ministry division of Indianapolis Youth for Christ. This was a time of intense learning so my abilities and skills increased and I had to learn the ins and outs of Christian organizational politics.

III. GROWING INFLUENCE

A. Seminary

Note how the narrative of this SnapShot was written to correlate with the titles in the Personal Timeline.

While work with the kids in the Clubhouse was rewarding and a great deal of growth took place learning to direct the Urban Ministry programs for Youth for Christ Indianapolis, a desire remained for more education. Now married, my wife and I applied to Fuller Theological Seminary in Pasadena, CA and upon acceptance, were off to a new adventure and phase in our lives.

Once I it was known that I had been accepted by Fuller Seminary and was planning to attend, the National office Youth For Christ approached me to represent the organization in a special training program being done in conjunction with the Young Life organization. Fuller called the program its Urban Youth Ministry Project and for my participation, I would be given the title of Senior Staff Intern for the Seminary and be personally supervised by Dr. William E. Pannell, a seminary professor and noted African American evangelical leader.

The Fuller Urban Youth Ministry Project lasted for five years. During the course of the project I completed my Master of Divinity studies through the School of Theology and gained teaching experience at the graduate level. Dr. Pannell also became my mentor and friend and under his tutelage I grew in terms of professional experience and reputation.

B. L. C. W. E.

Following the conclusion of the Urban Youth Ministry Project, I enrolled in the School of World Missions and began studies in their leadership program. I also went to work for the Lausanne Committee for World Evangelization (LCWE) as their national director for ethnic leadership development. In that position I became responsible for working with the nations ethnic leaders of color to help them identify and grow their emerging leadership. Today, all of my gifts and abilities continue to converge and I recognize that God is using me for his kingdom.

The Formative Encounter

Focus in on the lesson and how the learning has affected you.

The development of your Formative Encounters is probably the most important aspect of your PSDA. It is through this portion of the study that you will see that God has never been absent from your journey.

There are four sections to the Formative Encounter. They are:

> The Demographic Section
> The Encounter
> The Interpretation
> The Spiritual Principle

This is one shaping event that may or may not span a large number of years.

SECTION ONE: The Demographic Section

Development Paradigm: *FOUNDATIONAL BASE*

**Pride in Faithfulness
(Grandma)**

Formative Encounter Type: Personal Discovery

Time: Age 11

Note the four sections that comprise the demographics of your formative encounter. They are:

(1) The Developmental Paradigm in which the encounter occurred (foundational base above).

(2) The Title of the encounter. This title should exactly match the title found in your Personal Timeline.

(3) The Type of encounter (personal discovery above)

(4) The Time or approximate age when the encounter took place. *Remember the encounters should flow chronologically.*

SECTION TWO: The Story of the Encounter

Stories flow from your own life's experiences!!

The Encounter:

Grandma taught me many things that I can only now appreciate. Many of the things she taught me were accomplished by her negative example rather than deliberate molding, even so, she did instill in me a pride in faithfulness and I am sure that she realized that she had done so.

My grandmother was a Godly woman. Often during the years I lived with her, I would see her pouring herself into the Word. She never shared with me about spiritual things, never told me what she was reading, never bought me a Bible, but she did make sure that I was in Sunday School and Church every Sunday. Also, she taught me to say a simple prayer each night before I went to bed.

"Now I lay me down to sleep, I pray the Lord my soul to keep. If I should die before I wake, I pray the Lord my soul to take."

It was all the prayer I knew and I recited it every night before going to bed. One Sunday morning in Sunday school, the teacher asked for a show of hands for everyone who prayed every day. I was the only one to raise my hand. The teacher just ignored me as though she didn't really believe me, but that was all right with me.

> SECTION THREE: What the Encounter means to you

Interpretative Comment: *(How did the Encounter impact who you are today?)*

Even at that young age, I knew for myself that I was sincere and received a sense of personal satisfaction in knowing that I had been faithful. It didn't matter to me that I wasn't believed.

How has this encounter shaped how you are today in terms of the "beingness" of who you are.

(You should be able to identify a spiritual principle that applies to everyone.)

> SECTION FOUR: A Universal principle

Spiritual Application or Principle:

Bring up a child in the way that he should go and when he is old he will not depart from it.

What is the universal principle or truth that flows from the Encounter?

Here is an example of a completed Formative Encounter

Development Paradigm: *Foundational Base*
Title: *Pride in Faithfulness (Grandma)*
Formative Encounter: *Personal Discovery*
Time: Age 11

The Encounter:

Grandma taught me many things that I can only now appreciate. Many of the things she taught me were accomplished by her negative example rather than deliberate molding, even so, she did instill in me a pride in faithfulness and I am sure that she realized that she had done so.

My grandmother was a Godly woman. Often during the years I lived with her, I would see her pouring herself into the Word. She never shared with me about spiritual things, never told me what she was reading, never bought me a Bible, but she did make sure that I was in Sunday School and Church every Sunday. Also, she taught me to say a simple prayer each night before I went to bed.

"Now I lay me down to sleep, I pray the Lord my soul to keep. If I should die before I wake, I pray the Lord my soul to take."

It was all the prayer I knew and I recited it every night before going to bed. One Sunday morning in Sunday school, the teacher asked for a show of hands for everyone who prayed every day. I was the only one to raise my hand. The teacher just ignored me as though she didn't really believe me, but that was all right with me.

Interpretative Comment:

Even at that young age, I knew for myself that I was sincere and received a sense of personal satisfaction in knowing that I had been faithful. It didn't matter to me that I wasn't believed.

<u>Spiritual Application or Principle:</u>

Bring up a child in the way that he should go and when he is old, he will not depart from it.

The Various Types of Formative Encounters

In his book *Making of a Leader*, Dr. Clinton offers a large variety of what he terms "Process Items." He also offers the developmental phase in which a given process item should occur. For the PSDA, you should identify those items that have been meaningful (formative) for you spiritually. Your conversion to Christ would be one example of a spiritually "Formative" encounter. Other spiritually "Formative" encounters you might consider:

- Death Check
- Baptism
- Church
- Testimony
- Marriage
- God in nature
- Discovery
- Etc.

God wants each of us to grow and uses our relationship with Him and our life experiences to help in that growth process.

6

The Discovery Statement

Once you have completed your Timeline, SnapShot and Formative Encounters, end the study with a two or three paragraph reflection which focuses on what you have learned about how God has been using the events of your life to mold and shape you into the spiritual being you are becoming, this is *The Discovery Statement*. Also include how the execution of this project affected you at this point in your development.

The following is an example of a Discovery Statement.

As I write this final observation, I am exhausted. I found writing my own personal spiritual development analysis to be one of the most difficult projects of my experience. Part of the difficulty lie in the fact that the study is so personal. I also regret not having had the time to contribute two or three Formative Encounters every week so that I would not have had to do 90% of the work over the last week.

This study has helped me to look into my past. Sometimes it wasn't easy to write about the hard things in my life. But other times when I could see where God was in certain events, people and places, it helped increase my faith.

I hope to expand this study in the future. I love writing and reflecting on what God has done in my life and I am excited to see what he has in store for me. I know that with God, it will be worth it.

7

Sample PSDA

Personal Spiritual Development Analysis

Of

Name was inserted here

Date

Expanded Personal Biography

Date information compiled for study: Spring of 2010

Name: Gifted Student

Current Age: 27

Personal Timeline Dates: 3/29/83

Date Study Was Completed: April 2010

Age When I Embraced Jesus Christ As Savior: Teenager

Age When I Discovered My Spiritual Gifts: 19

Spiritual Gifts Mix:

Primary Gift: Teaching
Secondary Gift: Administration
Secondary Gift: Pastoring/Shepherding
Secondary Gift: Exhortation

Talents:

Primary Talent: Teaching
Secondary Talent: Public speaking
Major Roles I've Occupied: Student, pastor, father, son, brother, husband.

Personal Timeline

Hard Times	Looking Up	Moving On
1987	2005	2008
A "Prevenient Grace" B "The Fear of the Lord"	A "Real Conversion" B "Growth"	A "Purgatory" B "Fresh Air"
1	18	21
A. Maybury, KY B. Elizabethtown, KY	A/B. City, KY	A. Jamestown, KY B. Sonora, KY
A1 Baptism A2 Kicked Out A3 The Rocket A5 New Home B1 Conversion B2 The Move B3 Amy B4 Church Dating B5 Pregnant B6 Fallout B7 "Real Conversion" B7 My Call	A1 Marriage A2 City A3 Mary A4 Grocery Baskets B1 College B2 Another One, and Nowhere to Live B3 The Pinnacle B4 Toronto	A1 Pleasantville A2 The Letter A3 "This is Stupid" B1 Sonora B2 Seminary

The Snapshot

1. Hard Times
a. "Prevenient Grace"

I would have denied it at the time, but even a brief recapitulation of my life to this point makes it quite apparent that God has gone on before me. Even in the moments of my life when the thought of any sort of "higher power" seemed ridiculous, much less a personal, powerful Lord we know as Jesus the Christ, God was still present. It was in this period of my life from age 1 to 10, that I had no real relationship with God, and my life circumstance precluded me from any sort of reflection on the notion of a god. I grew up in Maybury, KY. I was baptized within a few months of being born, an act of submission and obedience on the part of my parents and home church that I'm greatly appreciative of now.

I grew up extremely poor. A lack of food, welfare, and a general sense of worthlessness characterized this period of my life. We lived in mobile home with no heat or air, leaky pipes, and infested with mice and roaches. My clothes all came from Goodwill or the United Methodist Mountain Mission. At age 7, my paternal grandfather from whom we "rented" the mobile home decided that he wanted the space that the home rested on for a garage. He quickly kicked us out. Fortunately, my maternal grandparents were much more loving and quickly took us in until we could find another home. What was intended to be a short stay of about a week or so ended up being a two-year ordeal.

It was at this time that school life became hellish for me. One particular incident that rises above others of this time, involved a "do-it-yourself rocket" kit. My fourth grade science class was to pay twenty dollars apiece in order to secure a rocket. Twenty dollars was an enormous amount at the time, an amount we did not have. I was literally the only child in the fourth grade that didn't have a rocket. While I can't remember anybody specifically antagonizing me, the silent stares said quite enough.

However, if there was any consolation from this time, it came in the form of government housing provided for low-income families. We received one of these homes in a neighborhood in which many of school friends lived. This experience helped me to see that I wasn't the only "poor kid" in school. It also gave me great pride to have an actual home.

b. "The Fear of the Lord"

It was at this time, in our new home, that I began to ponder the existence of God. My maternal grandfather was a United Methodist minister, so I had heard plenty about God. I knew intellectually that I was supposed to believe in God. It was at this time that I gave my life to God...I think. I was so afraid that if I did not say the "sinner's prayer" that I would burn in the fires of hell. At eleven years old, Mom and Dad said we were moving schools. Being people with little education at the time, they went where the jobs were and at this point in my life the jobs weren't in the county where I had attended school since second grade. I was furious, afraid, and looking back I think I went through a very real period of minor depression.

The move was very rocky. I distinctly remember not having a friend for at least six months. It was one of the loneliest periods of my life. However, I met a girl in my math science classes that I found intriguing. I was enraptured with her personality and beauty. We became "boyfriend" and "girlfriend" which helped my popularity immensely. Amy was well established on the popularity totem pole. In order to be able to see each other (her parents were very strict about dating) we began to go to church together. Neither of us cared about church at all, but we liked seeing each other and God was working through this even though we didn't know it.

Amy and I became sexually active. We had no relationship with the Lord and didn't really want one either. In our senior year, while we were both seventeen years old, she became pregnant with our daughter, Emily. We were terrified. The fallout from the pregnancy was horrendous. Amy's parents all but disowned her and my parents were in a state of shock. The fallout ended with a court "battle" between Amy and I and her parents over the issue of marriage. We wanted to marry. We were young but we loved each other. Looking back I see how naïve we were about marriage, our age, and our own maturity. The judge let us marry and while this could have easily been a catalyst for years of resentment and anger on both sides, God immediately began the healing process with the birth of our daughter. There's something about a baby that brings people together. It's hard to be mad while holding new life. It was also at this time that I truly became converted to Christ Jesus. Furthermore, in the midst of this anger and pain, God clearly called me to ministry. All most over night I fell madly in love with God. The pain of my past and the fear of my future faded as I contemplated God and His goodness. It was at this time that I felt called to serve God. Ironically (or perhaps not ironically in light of prevenient grace) God had called Amy as well. Amy didn't feel that she was called to pastor, but felt that God had called her to be a nurse and serve within the local church in some capacity. God was already working on Amy before I had a chance to get to her, go figure!

2. Looking Up
a. "Real Conversion"

In the midst of the birth of Emily and trying to finish high school, I was offered to serve a church in a small town on the edge of the Ohio River. After prayer and reflection, I accepted and became the pastor of City United Methodist Church.

What wonderful people they were! City had had many student pastors in the past and they had learned to be people of grace and understanding. One such woman of grace was Amy Bradford, affectionately called "Mary" because of her small stature.

Mary was my biggest cheerleader within the church and assumed that all I said was gospel. She consistently defended me when people opposed my ideas. Mary died of brain cancer. She had a rapid decline in health and died quickly. Her death absolutely broke my heart.

Mary's passing was my first lesson about ministry: ministry is hard and painful. So much about her death caused me to question much of my theology and understanding about God. This was a major growing period for me. My next lesson came shortly thereafter. Every year at Christmas, City bought baskets of groceries for the poor in the area and hand delivered them while singing carols. At the administrative meeting in which we delegated funds for this project, one woman complained that the money we give and the groceries we provide is unappreciated and thus we should stop the program. This was my next major lesson: ministry often involves people who don't understand "kingdom" ethics or economics.

b. "Growth"

It was also at this time (age eighteen) that I began my studies in college. College produced a major paradigm shift for me. I went a Christian college but I was immediately introduced to atheists, liberals, and all sorts of other "evils" (tongue planted firmly in cheek). I had never been around so many new sorts of people and ideas. It was in my sophomore year that Amy became pregnant once more. Life was hard enough as it is, another child only exacerbated the problem. In addition to this news, we found out that my maternal grandparents, with whom we'd lived with since we were married at eighteen, were moving and we'd have to find another place to live. I experience a second major depression in my life. I couldn't eat, sleep, or think straight.

My campus minister suggested that I go on a mission trip with the college ministry group to The Pinnacle, MS. I reluctantly agreed. On the trip I experienced my first real encounter with the Holy Spirit. I found healing by helping those who had been given a very hard road to walk. At the final worship service on the night before we were to depart and go back to KY, I was overcome with emotion and I felt a calm assurance that I had never experience before in my entire life. Following this experience, I consistently looked for mission opportunities. One such opportunity allowed me to go to Toronto to do inner-city mission work. This was my first real experience with the extremely impoverished as well as homosexuals. It was a time of stretching for me, as I learned to cope with the understanding that some people have extremely difficult lives and as a Christian, I'm called to speak healing into that life.

3. Moving On
a. "Purgatory"

As our family grew, our small church and the small salary it offered was no longer viable as an employer. We loved the church but were having great difficulty paying bills. I was then moved to a larger church in Jamestown, KY. I served this church for one year; it was one of the worst years of my life. My wife and I jokingly refer to this period of our life as "purgatory". The church was full of strife, anger, and dysfunction. Worse yet, they didn't realize it and became upset when you tried to speak to it. One such incident involved a man writing an angry letter to the entire church and distributing it throughout the congregation because he was upset over how $217.00 was spent. This letter nearly split the church in half. Meanwhile, my marriage and health were being rent asunder.

Perhaps the last straw for me personally, came the Sunday before Easter. This church had settled into the practice of having a sunrise service, but no 11 a.m. service on Easter. While I love sunrise services, I felt that there was quite a need for an 11 a.m. service as well. After all, many people only come to church on Easter, and I didn't want us to miss out because our doors were locked at 11 a.m. Most people were fine with adding an 11 a.m. service, but there was a minority contingent who did not like it because it was against "tradition". They never could see outside of their own walls to understand that the service was added not for them, but for those outside the four walls. The antagonism culminated with a woman looking at me and saying, "This new service is just stupid." Stupid? Really? Amy and I knew we had to leave, it did us no good to cast pearls among the swine.

Formative Encounters

Formative Encounters

Development Paradigm: Hard Times
Title: Baptism
Formative Encounter Type   Prevenient Grace
Time: Age 1

The Encounter

This entire past year can be characterized by being "a breath of fresh air". Amy and I moved to a new church that is intensely aware and focused upon the needs of its community. Furthermore, I began seminary. I've always been one who has loved school and academia. At seminary, I've found a niche, a comfort zone that has allowed me to heal from my past year in "purgatory". I've met new people from different traditions and it's been a refreshing year to say the least. Now I'm simply waiting to see where God leads me next.

I would be lying if I said I remembered my baptism. However, the effects of that baptism are evident in my spiritual journey and in my life. My parents felt it necessary to baptize me at a young age for several reasons. First, our faith tradition places great value on the baptism of children and infants. We believe the Gospel is for all people of all ages and as such, all ages are permissible for the sacrament. Second, we truly believe baptism does something. That is, we don't see baptism as symbol alone, although it is a symbol. Through baptism we acknowledge the work that God is doing in the person.

Recapitulating my life leads me to see countless times where God's grace has gone on before my heart and my mind. It's often taken me a while to see God's goodness and work in my life, even though it was present all along. Baptism is one such time for me. The effects of that day have been present ever since in my devotion to the Lord, my constant communion with the Spirit and God's showing of Himself to me.

Interpretive Comment

Even at this young age, God was already at work in me, even though I didn't know it. Today I try to be more aware of God's grace and presence in my life.

Spiritual Application

God's grace is present in all people, even if they're unaware of it at the time.

Developmental Paradigm: Hard Times
Title: Kicked Out
Formative Encounter Type: Spiritual "Stretching"
Time: Age 7

The Encounter

At age 7, my paternal grandfather, whom we rented a mobile home from, kicked my family out. I remember coming home from school one afternoon to find a few boxes of our most "essential" possessions setting by the door as my mother and father screamed at each other in anger, panic, shock, and misguided anger. The mobile home we lived in had no heat, no air, and the pipes often leaked or froze. We lived on food, handouts and the grace of God. My mother and father went from job to job, always looking for better pay.

My paternal grandfather is a man of purpose selfishness. When he sees something he wants or he believes he needs, he simply goes and get it, regardless of the consequences his actions may have on those around him. My grandfather decided that the trailer we lived in was eye sore and that plot of ground would be better served as a garden. In order to save face, he told my parents that he needed for them to pay rent to him in order to stay. He told them this at a time when we barely ate, much less could afford rent. When my parents stated the truth, that we couldn't pay, he kicked them out. He justified his actions by stating that he was trying to be fair and let us pay rent, and he was only kicking us out because he had to. This day is etched into my heart and my memory. I can't get rid of the feeling I had in my stomach. I was literally homeless.

Thankfully, my maternal grandparents took us in and gave us a home. By the grace of God we were able to live with them for a year as we attempted to get our life in order.

Interpretive Comment

I learned quickly that the only "person" we can truly count on is the Lord Himself.

People, even those who are very close to us, will at times let us down. It is better for humankind to place its trust in God than humanity.

Spiritual Application

God is faithful to us at all times, even when those around us are not faithful to us.

Development Paradigm: Hard Times
Title: The Rocket
Formative Encounter Type: Painful Experience
Time: Age 10

The Encounter

This is perhaps one of my most painful memories. In fourth grade the entire science class put together a "rocket launch." For twenty dollars, each student would receive a rocket kit which we would build and eventually launch. All of us were so excited. However, twenty dollars to my family may as well have been a million dollars. We were living rent-free with my grandparents still and we could barely afford to help them pay for groceries.

I assumed that I wouldn't be the only kid without a rocket. The town we lived in offered little employment so many kids were in the same boat I was in. However, I really was the only kid who didn't have a rocket. While the other kids constructed their rocket in class, I was given an "alternate" assignment. The embarrassment was so painful, even to this day I can't shake that memory from my mind. Perhaps there is a life lesson in this story about perseverance, pain, and justice. But for a young fourth grader, this experience only made my cynical, embarrassed, and ashamed.

Interpretive Comment

Our entire life we're told to be fair and act out of an acute sense of right and wrong. Nevertheless, the truth about life is that many of experiences and encounters are not "fair" or even just. Ultimately, justice and fairness won't come to fruition until the return of the Messiah.

Spiritual Application

Only in Christ is there true fairness and justice. Nevertheless, I shouldn't have been left to be the only kid in fourth grade with no rocket. Thus, someone should have stood up for me. We are all called to stand up for the poor, oppressed, and disenfranchised.

Development Paradigm: Hard Times
Title: New Home
Formative Encounter Type: Blessing
Time: Age 11

The Encounter

My entire life up to this point had been characterized by poverty and struggle. However, this short period of my life gave me a respite. We moved into what most people would call the "projects", government run housing. However, unlike the projects in large cities, these were actual houses which gave me and my family a feeling of respectability, as if we were actually accomplishing something.

For years we had lived at the expense and mercy of our family and others. This government housing actually had a very low rent which made my mother and father feel like they were actually providing us with something. Furthermore, the back yard was massive, and I do mean massive. It was a young boy's dream I was able to have large-scale football games in the back yard with my friends. For the first time in my life, things were beginning to look up.

Interpretive Comment

In the most trying time in life, it's essential that we remember that God is still present and sometimes we're simply called to endure and persevere. This is never popular or easy. And yet biblically, God allows for the Church and those he has special missions for to suffer. The key to life is endurance in the face of odds and opposition.

Spiritual Application

Life is never easy. If we are to succeed and live with any semblance of joy or happiness, we must be able and willing to endure.

Development Paradigm: Hard Times
Title: Conversion
Formative Encounter Type: Spiritual Discernment
Time: Age 11

The Encounter

When I was eleven years old, I distinctly remember have a great fear of God. Television and my Gideon's KJV bible made me acutely aware of my sin and depravity.

From a very young age I understood God as mean, vengeful entity up in the sky that watched over my every move waiting to pounce when I messed up. The more I heard about hell and the possibility that I might go there, I knew I had to "get saved".

I remember setting in a chair in my room, praying over John 3:16, asking God to forgive me for my horrid behavior. I hadn't done any more wrong than an eleven year-old boy could do, but I was convinced that I was going straight to hell. From that time on, I used to tell people that it was at that moment that I "got saved." It wasn't until I was older that I began to understand salvation as a process and that God was not as angry at me as I had thought. To this day, grace plays a very large role in my theology because I now understand the power and overwhelming determination that God uses to reach his children.

Interpretive Comment

We do not serve an angry, vengeful God, we serve a God that is full or mercy and grace. It took me many years to understand this concept, but God was gracious enough to show me his grace at work in many areas of my life.

Spiritual Application

God seeks to know us and know us well. As such, he comes to us as a loving father and not as angry boss or disciplinarian.

Development Paradigm: Hard Times
Title: The Move
Formative Encounter Type: Spiritual "Stretching"
Time: Age 12

The Encounter

After becoming somewhat established in my school following our move into the "projects", my mother and father both received jobs in another county. We couldn't afford to actually move to the new county, so my mother and father commuted. As such, my brother and I had no choice but to transfer schools to the county where my parents worked. This allowed them to drive us to school and pick us up when work was over. This was devastating to me. I'm naturally somewhat shy, so for me to have to start completely over and make an entirely new stable of friends is quite a daunting task.

When we moved, I immediately fell into the crowd of kids that often found themselves on the receiving end of ridicule. I was the "new guy" and the popular kids let me know it. It was the loneliest time of my life. For six months I made no friends and spent most of my day in fear of being ridiculed in front of my peers. This was one of the hardest periods in my life. During the first six months at this new school, I barely spoke to anyone and I kept my head down when I walked. This was also the time when puberty was doing its best to embarrass me. My voice cracked regularly, I had acne, and I was generally awkward.

I see now that this experience helped me to learn how to cope with new situations and new people. Furthermore, this move ended up being a great thing in my life.

Interpretive Comment

Life is an ever evolving and changing experience. A person must be able to adapt and cope with new environments, situations, and people.

Spiritual Application

In life, as well as in ministry, we are exposed to change almost constantly. We must be able to cope and adapt to these changes.

Development Paradigm: Hard Times
Title: Amy
Formative Encounter Type: Blessing
Time: Age 12

The Encounter

Although I had experienced six months of torment at my new school, things began to turn around when I met a girl named Amy. Amy and I got along quite well. Both of us were concerned about our grades, both of us had similar classes, and both of us found the other attractive. Amy was well established at school. Her family was active in booster organizations and Amy was quite popular. I had no idea why she would be interested in a poor "new guy" that no one else seemed to care about at all.

Amy and I began to spend more and more time together, and like all pubescent teenage boys, I thought I was in love. Looking back, I realize how true that sentiment was. I loved her with a passion and she returned the favor. Amy literally changed my life. All of a sudden, I was no longer the new guy that no one liked; I was part of the "in-crowd". Amy introduced me to many new people and opportunities. Amy eventually became my wife. We've been "together" since eight grade. It's important to note that I wouldn't be with her if God had listened to me. I didn't want to move, but without moving I would have never met my wife.

Interpretive Comment

God is always in control, even when it doesn't feel like it. Without God's providence in the decision for my family to move, I would have never met my future wife. While it required me to endure some trying times, God had a plan that I wasn't aware of at the time.

Spiritual Application

God's providence is always present and we're often unaware of it.

Development Paradigm: Hard Times
Title: Church Dating
Formative Encounter Type: Spiritual "Stretching"
Time: Age 13 - 16

The Encounter

Amy's parents were absolutely against Amy and I dating in almost any form. We weren't allowed to go anywhere without a stable of people around us to watch over us. In order to get around this, I invited Amy to church. My grandfather is a United Methodist minister so church was an easy and seemingly innocent way for Amy and I to see each other. Furthermore, Amy's parents were okay with church, so we were able to go by ourselves. However, it was at this time that we began to be sexually active.

Sometimes Amy and I would skip church and go off by ourselves. We resented the lack of trust that Amy's parents had for us, but in the process of rebelling, we were doing the very thing that confirmed their lack of trust. In the midst of this though, we did go to church sometimes. Amy began to ask me questions about God and salvation. She had grown up pseudo-Catholic and she assumed that I knew a lot about Christ because of my grandfather. But I had no real relationship with God. So we decided to learn together. In the midst of our sin, God was calling us closer and preparing our hearts to do some awesome work.

Interpretive Comment

Even in our sin God was pulling us toward himself. He pursued us with reckless abandon.

Spiritual Application

God can even use our sin to bring us to Him. Through our rebellion God speaks to us, not wishing for us to reject him.

Development Paradigm: Hard Times
Title: Pregnant
Formative Encounter Type: Crisis
Time: Age 18

The Encounter

Our senior year of high school was the most trying time of my life. This encounter epitomized the title of this development paradigm. Amy became pregnant. Amy and I were terrified about what the outcome may be. We loved each other, that really was true, but we weren't naïve. Neither of us had jobs or an ample amount of maturity to raise a child. Despite our fears, Amy and I pulled together. We decided that the only right thing to do was to get married (even though we had no clue where we'd live). I got a night job and began working and saving up money. However, Amy's parents had other plans.

Interpretive Comment

This was just a very difficult time in our life. It created a paradigm shift for us. We felt as helpless as two people could ever be.

Spiritual Application

God gave me a daughter from my sin. This was the second major time in my life when God used my sin and turned it around for his glory.

Development Paradigm: Hard Times
Title: The Fallout
Formative Encounter Type: Crisis
Time: Age 18

The Encounter

Amy and I wanted to marry. We felt that this was the proper response to our sin and this crisis. However, Amy's parents nearly lost their mind. Although they had known me for 5 years, they treated me as though I was a criminal. I never denied that what I had done was wrong, but you would have thought I was dodging my responsibility by the way they treated me. Amy's parents wanted to file an injunction that kept me away from the child.

This whole fight put an enormous amount of stress on us both, so much so that we were worried about Amy's health. Finally, after much research and anguish, Amy and I decided to petition a judge to allow us to get married even though her parent's didn't consent. One morning we met at school, skipped our classes and went to the courthouse. We had a prearranged meeting with him. We were so naïve. We thought we could convince him to let us marry and our parents would never know. To our horror, he said that he was going to call our parents in individually and speak to them.

After two months the judge called us all in for his decision. He was going to allow us to marry. I've never felt such relief in all my life. However, I feared that the chasm between myself and my future in-laws was too great to overcome. Not so. God slowly but surely allowed us to begin healing. Today, I have a good relationship with my in-laws. I would be lying if I said we were best pals but we do get along fine and we care for each other. God is good.

Interpretive Comment

This was the single hardest time in my entire life. I was so elated when the judge allowed us to marry. All I knew was that I loved my wife and I loved this unborn child and I wanted to be a good husband and father. Under most circumstances I would never have been able to fix the broken relationship I had with my in-laws, but God allowed it to be so.

Spiritual Application

Even when the world says there is no way healing can be accomplished, God is still the great Healer.

Development Paradigm: Hard Times
Title: Real Conversion
Formative Encounter Type: Conversion
Time: Age 18

The Encounter

At age seventeen, right before Amy and I found out we were pregnant; I started to become closer to God. While I was still living in sin, I did have an acute desire to grow closer to the God I had abandoned many years before. I was still somewhat afraid of God and his wrath, but I was beginning to change my mind about this God. I expressed my interest to my grandmother and she was thrilled. While driving me home one day she stopped at a LifeWay book store and bought me a NIV Study Bible. This was my first experience outside of the KJV.

I couldn't believe what the study boxes said on the pages. God was loving? God wants me? This Bible literally led me to Christ. I will forever be thankful for that Bible and for my grandmother's willingness to buy it for me. One night, in the bathtub of all places, I honestly gave my life to Christ. Scales didn't fall from my eyes and there wasn't an earthquake or choir of heavenly hosts, but I knew that my life had honestly turned the corner and I actually knew God in some way.

Interpretive Comment

My moment of justification was a momentous moment in my life. However, it was only the beginning of my spiritual walk. Since then God has been at work in my sanctification, moving on towards perfection.

Spiritual Application

While I view salvation as a process, there is a moment when the heart turns. Sometimes the process is so gradual that the actual moment is not perceptible, but it is there nonetheless.

Development Paradigm: Hard Times
Title: My Call
Formative Encounter Type: Calling
Time: Age 18

The Encounter

At eighteen, following my true conversion, I felt called to ministry. I told Amy and to my surprise, she felt the same way about nursing. She had grown closer to God as well and it was clear that God was calling us both to local ministry but in different venues. At first, I resisted my call, but after God's consistent urging and pursuance, made it clear to me that I wouldn't be happy doing anything else. I wanted a career with prestige and money, instead, God called me to a life of service with very little chance of monetary wealth.

I was obedient to my call (eventually) and began the ordination process for the United Methodist Church. Today, I'm a licensed pastor seeking ordination as I finish seminary here at Asbury.

Interpretive Comment

God changed my priorities and career path completely. Fortunately, my wife was completely on board because God had done the same for her.

Spiritual Application

God's calling comes to all sorts of people in all sorts of life situations. Our responsibility is to be obedient to that call and fulfill it to the best of our ability.

Development Paradigm: Looking Up
Title: Marriage
Formation Encounter Type: Marriage
Time: Age 18

The Encounter

Everyone has this preconceived idea of marriage that it is happy and the husband and wife always get along, but this is not true. Marriage has numerous bumps in the road that a husband and wife must overcome together. Our marriage was bumpy in the beginning due to the previous stress of having our first child. When I thought of marriage I thought of Amy and I living in our own house together. Now we were living in the basement of my grandparents' house trying to finish high school.

Amy and I had trust issues not just between each other but with one another's parents as well. Both of us had a lot of healing to go through. God grace was with us the whole time. And while we fought the whole time it seemed we were becoming stronger as we faced obstacles together.

Interpretive Comment

We were learning to rely on God through difficult times in our marriage. The first year was difficult but God has made his presence and is continuing to heal us.

Spiritual Application

Relationships are not as easy as everyone wants to believe they are. Marriage is a lasting covenant between a man and woman that takes time and maturation with Gods' grace.

Development Paradigm: Looking Up
Title: City
Formation Encounter Type: Calling
Time: Age 18

The Encounter

City United Methodist Church was a small local church right by the banks of the Ohio River. The people of this church were very loving and welcoming. At our first visit to the church everyone welcomed us with open arms. They expressed their joy at having a "young" preacher and his family. This was our first appointment and God was clearly seen at work among the people of this congregation.

While our salary was low, this church was a place of healing for us. The congregation accepted that we were young parents and helped us grow in our spiritual journey. Furthermore, my age never seemed to be a hindrance to my ministry. Even though I was inexperienced the congregation was willing to accept when I made mistakes or wrong decisions. There were a few key people in the church that took time to teach me patience and care for a congregation. I am forever grateful for that little church on the river.

Interpretive Comment

My family and I were so excited to be serving a church. We still had so much to learn, but we had open hearts and open minds. God had placed us in a church that would allow us to grow by making mistakes and loving our congregation.

Spiritual Application

There are many times in your life that God leads you to places that you would never have thought you would be. And often those are places of great grace and promise.

Development Paradigm: Looking Up
Title: Mary
Formative Encounter Type: Spiritual Growth
Age: 18

The Encounter

Mary was a nickname for Amanda Bradford, she was a key member at City UMC. She was a helpful member of the community and very well respected. Every Sunday after worship she always told me how great the sermon was and how much she loved having me at City. Mary was a woman that after talking to for just a few minutes you could see God working through her. Her husband never attended church, but I attempted to minister to him through home visits. Even after numerous home visits her husband still did not attend church.

After a few months of being at City Mary was diagnosed with a massive brain tumor. Hearing this news was shocking not only to me, but the whole congregation. Every Sunday Mary came in with the best attitude even after she had been diagnosed She knew where she was going after she passed, to see her maker. While in class one day I received a phone call that Mary was in the hospital and had been receiving radiation and was very weak. I rushed to the hospital to be by her side. She aspirated and pneumonia set in and passed away within a few short hours. I was by her side when she passed and felt a calm reassuring presence in the room.

Her funeral was one of the hardest things I ever had to do. I barely got through the sermon. I felt honored to be able to do one last thing for Mary. This was first major lesson about ministry: it is hard and can be very painful.

Interpretive Comment

This was a very difficult experience for me, but one in which I grew greatly.

Spiritual Application

God calls us to grow close to people and this necessarily involves pain on some level.

Development Paradigm: Looking Up
Title: Grocery Baskets
Formative Encounter Type: Holy Frustration
Time: Age 19

The Encounter

Every year at Christmas City put together grocery baskets for the poor and gave gift cards or money to the poverty stricken families in the area. At the board meeting in which we decided how much money to give, one of the members suggested that we should not do the grocery baskets this year. This person's reasoning behind not doing the baskets was the possibility that people would use the money provided on cigarettes or alcohol.

I was enraged and bewildered. I could not believe that one of my own parishioners would suggest that we withhold much needed help. I managed to keep my temper down, however, I made it clear that God desired us to plant the seed, it's watering and growth were out of our hands. My point was, the Christian responsibility is to give freely, and pray for good stewardship on behalf of the recipient. This was my second major lesson in ministry: most people don't understand kingdom morality or kingdom economics.

Interpretive Comment

I realized at that point that my congregation's vision and my vision were very different and to be successful we would need to mesh together.

Spiritual Application

Much of ministry, and for that matter the Christian walk, is characterized by a counter/cultural ethic and worldview.

Development Paradigm: Looking Up
Title: College
Formative Encounter Type: Spiritual Growth
Time: Age 18 - 22

The Encounter

My undergraduate years were quite formative in the sense that I encountered new people, ideologies, and theologies. For the first time in my life I spent time with atheists and people outside of my comfort zone. I was astonished to find such an eclectic group of people at my small private college. This was a good experience for me because it forced me to rethink some of my previous assumptions and it reaffirmed many of my core believes about God, ethics and theology.

Within my major, Christian, Jews, agnostics, and atheists all dialogued together. This led too many fruitful discussions about pertinent issues of the day. While it was rare to come to a consensus within the group, we cared for each other and learned to respect each other's opinions and differences. This foundation has been helpful to me in my pastoral work as I am often introduced to people with differing views and ideologies from a post -modern culture that is always evolving.

Interpretive Comment

This is a great time of growth for me as I was placed in situations that I never would have been put in if I were not in college.

Spiritual Application

It's essential to be in dialogue with people and faith groups that differ from our own. While we may disagree, the conversation themselves can be fruitful.

Development Paradigm: Looking Up
Title: Another one, and Nowhere to Live
Formative Encounter Type: Mini Crisis
Time: Age 20

The Encounter

From the time our daughter was born my wife and I had lived with my grandparents in the basement of their parsonage. My grandfather being a United Methodist minister, it was always a risk he could be moved and my wife and I could be out of a home. In my sophomore year of college this fear came to fruition. My grandfather called us at school and said he was moving and that distance from the new parsonage and the college we were attending was too far to drive. Furthermore, Amy and I were pregnant again.

So within a month's time my wife and I had gone from one baby and no home of our own to one baby, one on the way, and no home. My wife and I panicked, but our faith in the Lord was much stronger this time than with our first child. So we sat out to do the most difficult task a Christian can do, wait on the Lord.

Interpretive Comment

This short period of time is characterized by fear and the exciting possibility of moving out on our own. However, we had to wait on God, which is a very difficult aspect of the Christian life.

Spiritual Application

At times our life seems as though were in limbo. As one door closes and one chapter ends were often left in the dark waiting for the light to shine from another room and the ink to be spilt on another chapter.

Development Paradigm: Looking Up
Title: The Pinnacle
Formative Encounter Type: Holy Spirit
Time: Age 20

The Encounter

As Amy and I waited for God to provide housing and the necessary income to live on our own I spent a day in the college chaplain's office bearing my soul and crying my eyes out. I just could not see where the money or the housing was going to come from. My chaplain suggested I attended a mission trip with a group of kids from the college to The Pinnacle, Mississippi. Hurricane Katrina had ravaged that town and a ton of work still needed to be done to help The Pinnacle. I figured that focusing all my energy on people with much greater problems than I would help my fear and put me in the right mind set.

The Pinnacle was exactly what I needed. The grace of those people and their appreciation for our service did my heart good. On the final night as twenty exhausted, but grateful college kids gathered around for one final devotion. I was overwhelmed with the presence of the Holy Spirit. My body tingled, I was overcome with emotion, and I felt an assurance that I have never before felt before or after. To my surprise, the rest of the group had the exact same experience. For one hour we sat and prayed for each other and basked in God's presence among us. For the first time in months I knew Amy and I were going to be ok. Shortly thereafter the housing and income became a reality.

Interpretive Comment

I had never, nor I have I sensed, felt the Holy Spirit in a palpable and powerful way. I look forward to experiencing it in this way again.

Spiritual Application

In order to comfort His children God often uses the ordinary, but transforms it to become the extraordinary. However, in some instances, as with my experience in The Pinnacle, God uses a much more and super natural manner to speak to us.

Developmental Paradigm: Looking Up
Title: Toronto
Formative Encounter Type: Spiritual Growth
Time: Age 20

The Encounter

Following The Pinnacle, I made it a priority to attend any mission trip that I could. One such mission trip came with a group of local youth to Toronto. The trip was centered around the inner city. It was the first time I had ever been close to homeless and extremely poor people. I was exposed to a whole new section of society that I thought only existed on television and in movies.

While in Toronto we were given an assignment that immersed us in the world of homelessness and poverty. The group leader said that the average homeless person in Toronto lived on less than 2 dollars a day. We were each given two dollars and were told to find shelter, food, and a place to use the restroom. For four hours I was homeless in a large city. I experienced firsthand the difficulties and embarrassment of begging for money and finding a place to facilitate simple human needs such as sleeping or using the restroom. I had already had a heart for the poor, but this was galvanized by desire to help the impoverished.

Interpretive Comment

I was amazed at how ashamed I felt to be homeless, even though I knew this was an exercise. This experience gave me a unique perspective into the life of extreme poverty.

Spiritual Application

In order to affectively minister to people sometimes you have to be more than near them, you have to live as they live.

Developmental Paradigm: Moving On
Title: Pleasant Grove
Formative Encounter Type: Holy Spirit
Time: Age 21

<u>The Encounter</u>

In order to help with our finances we moved from City UMC to Pleasant Grove UMC. This was a rather large salary increase for us and we were excited to be in a larger church with more resources. However, it quickly became apparent that this church had a history of dysfunction as well as a history of abusing pastors. I found every move that I tried to make as a leader was countered with opposition by a small group within the church. This small group of individuals had held the locus of power for many generations.

The constant conflict and struggle began to have negative effects on my health, marriage, school work, and my overall happiness. A point came in which I didn't even want to preach and several times I thought of quitting, but I knew this was not God's will.

My prayer quickly became for God to help me love these unlovable people.

<u>Interpretive Comment</u>

This was a very difficult time in my life because I began to question my call. It seemed to me that if God called me to do something it would come easily to me.

<u>Spiritual Application</u>

God often calls us to deal with people we do not like and place in situations which are very difficult. Nevertheless, we may be the vessel of grace for these people even if we are not aware of it.

Development Paradigm: Moving On
Title: The Letter
Formative Encounter Type: Conflict
Time: Age 21

The Encounter

I came to church one morning to find a disgruntled congregant making copies of a letter. As it turns out, this man was quite upset over how $217 dollars was spent. His Sunday school class had raised money for missions and decided to give a portion to a fund that was set up for parsonage repairs. This was voted on while he was away. While I disagreed with the allocation of the funds I felt that the Sunday school classes' intention was honorable even if mislead.

The letter he was copying, he planned to distribute throughout the church. He allowed me to read it. It was full of stinging attacks against different members of the church. I was completely taken aback by this and his unwillingness to talk to me about the issues. The fallout from this letter nearly split the church. From my previous ministry experience I had promised myself that I would handle conflict head on when it occurred and that is exactly what I did. The man decided to leave the church and while I was sorry to see him leave, his negative attitude and confrontational spirit were not missed.

Interpretive Comment

I dealt with a lot of conflict at Pleasant Grove, but this was the worse however I felt that God gave me wisdom to handle the situation as best as I could.

Spiritual Application

Sometimes for a community of believers to grow numerically or spiritually, pruning must be done so that those willing and able to bear fruit may bud forth.

Development Paradigm: Moving On
Title: This is Stupid
Formative Encounter Type: Opposition
Time: Age 21

The Encounter

It was the custom of pleasant Grove to have a Easter sunrise service, but no 1100 am service. While I had no problem with the sunrise service, I did have a problem with no 1100 am service. From my experience as a pastor I knew that Easter Sunday morning was a peak time for church attendance for many people visited family or made their annual pilgrimage to the church service. As such I didn't want us to miss out on reaching an un-church person.

My adding an 1100 am service was met with mixed reviews, as were all my decisions, but none as antagonistic as a woman named Roberta. One morning as I prepared to enter the pulpit to lead worship, Roberta asked me why I was messing with the church's tradition. I told her my logic to which she replied, "This is stupid," it was at this moment that I truly understood this church had no intention of dealing with people outside the four walls of the church.

Interpretive Comment

The blunt force of Robin's comment helped me to see that this church was heading for futility. Roberta's comment was only a microcosm of the overall church attitude.

Spiritual Application

Any deed done for the Lord will always be met with opposition from the world. If we are not being opposed by someone, than perhaps we need to get louder.

Development Paradigm: Moving On
Title: Sonora
Formative Encounter Type: New Beginning
Time: Age 22

The Encounter

I received a call one evening from my District Superintendent telling me that a church closer to seminary had come open. When asked if I was interested, I immediately answered in the affirmative. My D.S. stated the church was in Sonora, KY. Sonora was only miles from my wives family and only a fifteen-minute drive from mine.

While I wanted to tell my D.S. we wanted to go I knew that I had best pray on it. I was afraid that by saying yes, that I was merely running from our problems at Pleasant Grove. However, after much prayer and discussion with my wife we felt that this was a good opportunity and God was showing us a way out.

Since coming to Sonora my health and my stress level have both gotten much better. This is a church that is open and willing to reach out to the community. Since coming to Sonora we have began a community garden and have brought in several new families who were previously un-churched. It's wonderful to be with a group of people with the same goals as you do.

Interpretive Comment

Sonora is a breath of fresh air after a long and arduous year at Pleasant Grove.

Spiritual Application

God often rescues us from situations that stifle our gifts and calling.

Development Paradigm: Moving On
Title: Seminary
Formative Encounter Type: New Possibility
Age: 22

<u>The Encounter</u>

This is where I find myself today. Seminary is as great as I thought it would be. I enjoy the academic life, so seminary naturally fits me well. Even in my short time here I have met some fascinating people and have been introduced to new and richer theologies. I can already tell this experience is going to be extremely fruitful. This is a big shift for me. In one sense, a portion of my life is over: I'm done with college.

Seminary is all so very new and rewarding. I'm learning to expand my theology and see God in a much bigger, more cosmic way.

<u>Interpretive Comment</u>

Seminary is an experience pregnant with possibilities.

<u>Spiritual Application</u>

Every new experience has the possibility to be wonderful.

****

The Discovery Statement

This undertaking took quite a bit of time; however, it was quite interesting to see how God has been acting in my life for years. Even though this process is time consuming I would recommend it to my parishioners and other clergy. I never realized until I started putting the assignment together how many different times God had touched my life and changed it. This will be a file that I will add to as the year's progress and as God continues to work in my life. Now that the framework is set, adding events and editing my time line will be much easier.

Made in the USA
Middletown, DE
24 November 2020

25081575R00060